The laid-back wine guide

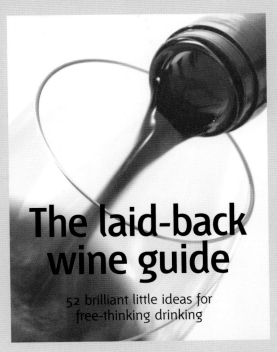

The laid-back wine guide

52 brilliant little ideas for
free-thinking drinking

Giles Kime

brilliantideas

CAREFUL NOW

Wine drinking should be enjoyable, but don't forget that wine is also an intoxicant which can damage your liver, your waistline – and your wallet. Please drink responsibly – apart from anything else, it's much more enjoyable when you can remember those delicious wines the next day.

Copyright © The Infinite Ideas Company Limited, 2008

The right of Giles Kime to be identified as the author of this book has been asserted in accordance with the Copyright, Designs and Patents Act 1988.

First published in 2008 by
The Infinite Ideas Company Limited
36 St Giles
Oxford
OX1 3LD
United Kingdom
www.infideas.com

A CIP catalogue record for this book is available from the British Library

ISBN 978-1-905940-41-7

Brand and product names are trademarks or registered trademarks of their respective owners.

Designed and typeset by Baseline Arts Ltd, Oxford
Printed in China

Brilliant ideas

Introduction

Unlike every previous book written on wine
this one won't tell you what you should think
about a wine. It will simply provide you with
the skills you need to make up your own
mind. To become a free-thinking drinker you don't need fancy
equipment and a small library of reference books, just...

- some very large, deep, tulip-shaped wine glasses with fine rims
- a knowledgeable, friendly wine merchant with whom you can
  develop a meaningful, lifelong relationship
- self-adhesive labels to indicate the identity of wines
- water biscuits to purge the palate
- a spittoon – a Champagne bucket is ideal
- a notebook to write your observations in
- a good wine atlas
- an open mind

Extensive tasting is the only way you'll ever deepen your
understanding of wine. Great tasters are not necessarily people who
are born with a special gift; they are simply people who are lucky
enough to have had the opportunity to taste a great many wines at
the same time.

However, tasting in a random way has only limited use. The suggested Taste Tests will enable you to compare one style of wine with another in a focused way. What is crucial to these tests is anonymity. Only when you have thoroughly examined every conceivable shade of difference between the wines should you reveal their identity. This second stage will offer yet another layer of interest.

Ideally, all the wines should be tasted in one sitting. If the wines are quite expensive it makes financial sense to share the tasting with another curious wine enthusiast. Most wines will keep for up to three days (and even longer if sealed under pressure in a preserving system). Conducting the test before and during a meal will not only make the occasion more enjoyable but also allow you to taste wine as part of a greater gastronomic experience – which in most cases is just as the winemaker intended and will have a significant impact on the flavour of the wine.

Because the availability of some wines is so patchy – and because they change from one year to the next – the suggestions are kept deliberately vague, e.g. cheap Australian Cabernet, good-quality white Burgundy. This is where a good wine merchant comes in. You need to find one who can understand what you are looking for and will then come up with a wine that is typical.

What you won't find in this book is any discussion of how one wine tasted against another. The wines rather than the pages are intended to speak for themselves.

1. Free your mind

If you usually open a bottle of wine burdened with preconceived ideas based on its label, its price and myths spun by the wine trade, it's time to learn the art of free-thinking drinking.

Many wine producers – especially those at the top end of the market – must have realised that confusion (or 'mystique' as they prefer to call it) can be used to commercial advantage. A bottle of wine can be sold for twice the amount of something comparable purely because it has a certain name or year on its label. Sadly, the result of the cult of mystique is likely to be a disheartened punter whose initial enthusiasm for wine is dampened by the fact that she can't remember the names of the top wines in the 1855 classification of Bordeaux or doesn't have an intimate knowledge of the topography of the Mosel Valley.

Here's an idea for you

The next time you open a bottle of wine, plot its origin as precisely as you can. You will find that rooting a wine in particular part of the globe will give the wine a context that makes it easier to understand.

Defining idea

'The only means of strengthening one's intellect is to make up one's mind about nothing – to let the mind be a thoroughfare for all thought.'
JOHN KEATS

Three steps to vinous enlightenment

Question everything. Don't accept anyone's word for anything. Most people who claim to be wine experts base their opinions on where a wine comes from, when it was made and what they have read about it. Just because a wine is served with great aplomb in a restaurant doesn't mean that you have to like it – though it's up to you whether you decide to express your opinion, particularly if someone else is paying.

Drink everything. The fact that you don't like a wine doesn't mean you shouldn't taste it. The more wines you taste, whether good or bad, the greater your frame of reference. However, for the sake of your liver, remember that there's a big difference between tasting and drinking.

Compare everything. A wine is defined by how it is similar to – or different from – another. It is these subtle shades of difference – between, say, an inexpensive red Bordeaux and a Chilean Merlot, an Australian sparkling wine and a bottle of vintage Bollinger, a Macon and a Chablis – that will reveal the true character of a wine.

2. The agony of choice

However wide the choice of wines on sale, only a relatively small number need concern the free-thinking drinker.

One of the secrets of free-thinking drinking is to start by reducing the number of wines in your radar. It's like the approach taken by a friend of mine to hefty weekend newspapers. She carries out a ruthless process she refers to as 'paper filleting'. First in the bin are the leaflets advertising garden furniture, then the finance and business sections and finally the sport – which leaves her with the news, arts and the colour supplement. Graduates of business school now refer to such a strategy as 'starting micro and going macro' (a philosophy that past generations might have described as 'not biting off more than you can chew').

Here's an idea for you

Take a scarily long list from your wine retailer and try to fillet it with a thick black marker – by crossing out either everything except for Bordeaux, Burgundy, the Loire, Australia and New Zealand or everything that isn't labelled Cabernet Sauvignon, Merlot, Pinot Noir, Sauvignon Blanc or Chardonnay. Suddenly the list looks less scary, doesn't it?

17

So how do you fillet a monster as vast and sprawling as the wine-producing regions? There are two different approaches; one for the classically minded, the other for the modernists. Both cover precisely the same ground but from two different perspectives.

The classical approach is geographical and encompasses three classic French wine regions – Bordeaux, Burgundy and the Loire – and two 'New World' regions: Australia and New Zealand. The modernist approach views the subject from the perspective of the world's five most successful grapes: Cabernet Sauvignon, Merlot, Pinot Noir, Sauvignon Blanc and Chardonnay.

Neither method is better than the other. The difference is not one of old buffers versus revolutionaries, but one of philosophy. Classicists believe that wine is primarily a product of the earth whereas modernists see it as a product of winemaking. There are convincing arguments for both perspectives. The truth, of course, is that wine is a product of both.

Whichever route you choose to follow, a good knowledge of the flavours and aromas associated with either the regions or the grapes will offer foundations on which to build a deeper understanding of wine. It will give you a key to a greater world beyond. Trust me.

3. Blind tasting

The quickest and most effective way to dispose of oenological baggage is to taste wines anonymously.

Blind tasting is an essential tool for ridding yourself of preconceptions based on the following:

1. Price. When we dig deeply into our pockets to buy a bottle of wine, we tend to be better disposed towards its contents – not least to justify our investment.
2. Origin. It may now be possible to make top-class wines in Uruguay, but most of us are still wedded to the idea that the world's finest wines come from the hallowed turf of Bordeaux, Burgundy and Champagne.
3. The image projected by a label. It's almost impossible not to be swayed by a well-designed label.

My suggestion is not that you only ever taste in this way but simply that you use blind tasting to give you a grounding in the tastes and flavours displayed by the wines you are studying. Make sure you have

Here's an idea for you

Blind tasting can become part of your life. Whenever anyone offers you a glass of wine, ask them not to reveal its identity until you have had a good chance to study it.

plenty of glasses. If you're tasting with a friend you'll need around twenty wine glasses, plus glasses for water. It's useful also to have water biscuits ready to occasionally purge your palate. It's a good idea to make notes under three headings: colour, aroma and flavour. Only when you've fully understood a wine should you reveal its identity.

A random selection of half a dozen red or white wines – not necessarily both colours at the same time – will give you an idea of the huge diversity of flavours and aromas. A selection of reds might include: red Bordeaux, Rhône red, red Burgundy, Australian Shiraz, New Zealand Pinot Noir and Chilean Cabernet. A selection of whites might include: white Loire, German Riesling, Australian Chardonnay, white Burgundy and New Zealand Sauvignon Blanc.

Start making specific comparisons between pairs of wines (without revealing their identities). At first the differences between one and the other will be hard to spot. Keep on coming back to the glasses and soon the distinctions will become clear. The fruity flavours of some wines may become apparent, while others may seem more sour. You might notice that some have a nutty smell, while others are more leafy. Whatever observations you make, it is important that they are your own.

4. Sweet dreams

Detecting sweetness in a wine shouldn't dampen your ardour – particularly when it's balanced with a good dose of mouth-watering acidity.

While some sweet wines can be disgusting others can be sublime. A slight hint of sweetness is an essential ingredient of some of the world's most successful wines and some of the world's most legendary, most expensive wines are really quite sweet.

If you need any proof that sweetness should not be a byword for lack of sophistication in a wine then you need only explore the wines of Sauternes and Chateau d'Yquem. The success of Yquem relies on exactly the same balance that explains the success of all really great sweet wines: it has sufficient acidity not to seem cloying and enough sweetness not to seem sour. This sounds simple but it's a surprisingly elusive quality.

Here's an idea for you

Pour half a bottle of sweetish German wine or Sauternes that is at room temperature into a decanter and put the remaining bottle in the fridge until it is lightly chilled. Next, compare the two. How does the temperature influence the flavour?

Defining idea

'Sweetness belongs in Mosel wines like bubbles belong in Champagne.'
NICK WEISS, Weingut St Urbanhoff

Many of the wines that wine drinkers regard as dry are, in fact, quite sweet. Much of the reason for the success of New World wines in the last decade is that they have a hint of tropical fruitiness that makes them far more approachable than the drier European wines they have eclipsed, such as Italian whites and Bordeaux reds. This distinction should be clear in the following simple Taste Test.

- White Rioja + cheap Champagne + inexpensive Australian Chardonnay + sweetish German Riesling
- Red Burgundy + inexpensive Australian Cabernet + Tawny Port + inexpensive Port

The reason that there are four wines in each line-up is to give a simple picture of the varying degrees of dryness and sweetness that can be found in wine. However, dryness or sweetness is not necessarily an indication of a wine's quality. What *is* key is the way dryness or sweetness is balanced with acidity. Any objective analysis of a wine should attempt to gauge the success of this balance. The presence of one without the other – or simply an imbalance between the two – can spell disaster.

5. Tasting tips

Understanding a wine's flavour is a much more complex art than you might imagine. But rest assured: with plenty of time, practice makes perfect.

The basic aim of tasting is to try to judge: the wine's acidity, sweetness, how well the sweetness and acidity are balanced, bitterness, how long any of these qualities stay in the mouth (known by wine buffs as their 'length').

You will need: suitable glasses, still mineral water, paper labels (if blind tasting), water biscuits, a large receptacle such as a Champagne bucket (if you are spitting), a notebook and pen.

Experiment until you find a tasting style that you feel happy with. But you might begin using the following procedure:

1. Hold up to the light and note the colour. Is it dense, pale or somewhere in between? You might also want to judge the

Here's an idea for you

Flavour and smell are two different things. To find out how the two are inextricably linked simply try the following test: taste a glass of wine that normally bursts with flavour and aroma while at the same time holding your nose. What more evidence do you need?

wine's viscosity, i.e. whether it leaves a transparent coating on the sides of the glass.

2. Next, swirl the wine around in your glass (to release its aroma) and then lower your nose into the glass, taking a deep breath that will collect the full effect of the wine's aroma. Don't even think about moving to the next stage until you have fully explored the scent – or lack of it – provided by the wine.

3. Now sip a small amount of wine, running it all over your palate, sucking a little air in after it.

4. Either swallow or spit. Some people feel that they haven't really tasted a wine until they have swallowed – although there are no taste buds in the throat, so technically it isn't necessary. Others find that even a hint of alcohol can dampen their objectivity.

5. Between wines it can sometimes be useful to clean the palate with water and/or a plain biscuit.

Defining idea

'If one can taste food, one can taste wine.'
MICHAEL BROADBENT

Note-taking is useful. Not only does it provide a record of wines that you have liked, it also forces you to focus on what you are tasting and to try to articulate your thoughts.

6. Good scents

The reason why wine offers such an enduring fascination is that it is one of the few liquids that can express such a complex range of aromas.

A surprising number of people rarely smell the wine they are drinking, with the result that they miss out on eighty per cent of its pleasure – particularly when drinking wine with fabulously aromatic qualities. The simple rule is never, ever to taste a wine without smelling it first. Only then will you begin to appreciate the wonderful array of aromas that wine can provide.

Beware of lists of grape varieties and their attributes. Free-thinking drinkers should cultivate the confidence to develop their *own* opinions about wine. If you're told that the typical aroma of Transylvanian Pinot Noir is 'sawdust from a hamster's cage', there's a danger that 'sawdust from a

Here's an idea for you

Try to get into the habit of never tasting a wine until you have fully explored its aroma. Make sure that you smell the wine and return to it three or four times before eventually letting it enter your mouth. This simple ritual will do a huge amount to accelerate your understanding of wine.

hamster's cage' is how you will perceive this aroma for evermore, even if a better analogy is 'dust from old floorboards'. Because wine is such a wildly subjective field, it is essential that you build up your own descriptive vocabulary. One taster's 'deliciously tropical fruit character' is another's 'smells horribly like Lilt'.

Instead of providing such a list, I'm going to suggest another tasting menu that will help you get to grips with the huge range of aromas offered by wine. When exploring the wines listed below, write down the names of other smells that they remind you of. Not all these wines have been chosen for their distinctive aroma – some are included simply to demonstrate the range of characters.

Aromatic whites: New Zealand Sauvignon, Gewurztraminer, German Riesling, Australian Chardonnay.

Scented reds: good-quality red Bordeaux, New Zealand Pinot Noir, good-quality Australian Shiraz, Australian Cabernet.

Having lined up your anonymous glasses of wine, allow yourself plenty of time to fully appreciate their aromas – and don't even think of tasting them until you have thoroughly explored how they differ from each other. Remember: the aromas of individual wines are defined by how they compare with one another.

7. Glass act

The perfect wine glass is much simpler – and cheaper – than you might be led to believe.

One's appreciation of the smell and flavour of a wine is influenced by the shape of the glass and the thickness of its rim. Take two glasses. The first glass should be the ubiquitous Paris goblet, with a modestly sized spherical bowl on a stem. The second glass must be larger and tulip-shaped, i.e. the circumference of the rim should be smaller than that of the bowl, and the glass must be thinner than in an everyday drinking glass. The test of good-quality glass is that it resonates when you flick it with a finger nail.

Pour about 125 ml of an aromatic white wine such as a good-quality New Zealand Sauvignon Blanc into each glass? In the smaller glass you will notice that the surface of the wine is much closer to the rim than in the larger glass, where it

Here's an idea for you

Try the Taste Test with other types of wine. How do the flavour and aroma of a good Fino Sherry compare when they are tasted in an old-fashioned thimble-sized Sherry glass, a tulip-shaped copita and a large wine glass? How does red Bordeaux vary when it is tasted in a tumbler and in a good-quality wine glass? Only extensive tasting will help you understand the complex relationship between a wine and the glass you drink it from.

occupies a relatively small proportion of the bowl. When you come to smell the wine, your nose will be much closer to the wine in the smaller glass than in the larger glass.

Ask yourself how the smell of the wine in the smaller glass compares with that of the wine in the larger glass. Is there any difference between the flavour of the wine in the small glass and flavour of the wine in the large glass?

There's no great mystery here: a large, tulip-shaped glass captures the aroma and if not overfilled will provide sufficient space for the wine to express itself. Combined with a thin rim – which is less intrusive in the tasting experience than a thick rim – it offers the ideal vessel in which to taste wine. Another obvious advantage of drinking wine from a tulip-shaped glass is that it allows you to swill the wine around in the glass without it spilling over the edges.

8. Chardonnay

Chardonnay is now so ubiquitous that for some people it has become something of a joke. Yet the grapes come in such great diversity that it is hard to generalise about them.

Depending on where it is grown, Chardonnay can demonstrate a huge variety of traits, from a steely, minerally austerity to a big, buttery richness. Like any grape it can also make wines that are extremely bland – and it is because of these that the better-quality examples have been given a bad name. But even when Chardonnay isn't well made it can still be much better than the basic examples of other white wines, such as Riesling or Sauvignon Blanc. It is perhaps this fact that has encouraged winemakers all over the world to make it their number one grape.

In the beginning there was Chablis, the most popular of all white Burgundies. Then the Australians

Here's an idea for you

Remember that when you are tasting the wines on the tasting menu you are doing so without food – or perhaps nothing more enticing than a dry biscuit. If possible, crank up your tasting session by trying the wines with food. Examine how the different styles combine with the flavours of spicy food, fish and red meat.

wanted a piece of the action and during the 60s and 70s Chardonnay became increasingly popular. The Californians planted it too and during the 80s and 90s it rapidly appeared in wine regions from Chile to South Africa. Chardonnay is now one of the most successful, widely recognised grape varieties, which winemakers love for its adaptability and drinkers for its approachability.

As with any grape variety the only way to find your way round all the different styles is to put your nose and palate to work. A good introduction should include: expensive Chablis, expensive Californian Chardonnay, inexpensive oaky Australian Chardonnay, unoaked Australian Chardonnay and Hungarian Chardonnay.

There were doubtless times in this Taste Test when you wondered whether you were tasting the same grape. Chardonnnay grown in the relatively chilly climes of Burgundy will inevitably have very different character from one grown in the sunny climes of New South Wales. But it isn't just the weather that affects the flavour of a wine. So too does the way that it is made. Ask yourself some of the following questions. Were some of the wines sweeter or drier than others? Stronger and more robust? A little more acidic? Slightly creamier? Fruitier?

9. Great whites

White wine doesn't begin and end with Chardonnay and Sauvignon Blanc. There are plenty of more obscure whites worth trying – some of them toe-curlingly unfashionable but nevertheless extraordinarily delicious.

Riesling. No longer fashionable, although plenty of delicious examples still abound, both from Germany and increasingly from other cool climate regions such as New Zealand.

Gewurztraminer. A sublimely scented wine whose spiritual home is in Alsace.

Pinot Grigio/Gris. The thin whites of northern Italy (known as Pinot Grigio) have done much to ruin the reputation of a grape that in the right hands can produce rich scented wines that make ideal partners to Asian food.

Semillon. The classic white grape of Bordeaux is now grown all over the world, notably in Australia, where it produces whites that put their French ancestors to shame.

Viognier. In the Rhône Valley, Viognier makes wines with an

Here's an idea for you

For a month challenge yourself to drink only white wines other than Chardonnay and Sauvignon Blanc. The more you taste around, the more happy discoveries you'll make.

almost mythical reputation. In the South of France and Australia it provides easy-drinking wines that make a good alternative to Chardonnay.

Verdelho. This obscure grape variety is now being used to make distinctive wines in Australia, particularly in the Hunter Valley in New South Wales.

Taste Test

• Australian Verdelho • Southern French Viognier • Good-quality Australian Semillon • New Zealand Pinot Gris • Good-quality Alsace Gewurztraminer • Good-quality dry Riesling • Good-quality Chardonnay • Good-quality Sauvignon Blanc.

You don't have to try all these wines at once. Four or five will suffice. The Chardonnay and Sauvignon have been included on the list so you have some familiar flavours and aromas to compare the more offbeat wines against. In each case consider the aroma, flavour, colour, how it might go with food and whether it would make a good aperitif.

The greater number of flavours and aromas you're aware of, the greater chance you'll have of finding wines that serve a specific purpose such as an aperitif or offer a good match with food, and the more bottles you have open at any one time, the more opportunities you'll have to compare them with different types of food – and with one another.

10. Grape expectations

Mastering the art of telling one grape from another is the easy bit. But, such is the intervention that goes on during the winemaking process, the *really* knotty question is whether grapes truly matter.

To demonstrate the diverse flavours that can be displayed by one grape variety, try a Taste Test on any of the following combinations:

- Burgundian Chardonnay + Australian Chardonnay
- Burgundian Pinot Noir + New Zealand Pinot Noir
- Loire Sauvignon Blanc + Chilean Sauvignon Blanc
- Sweet German Riesling + Australian dry Riesling

In most cases you will probably have found very different personalities demonstrated by the same grape and you might well be asking a question that is almost heretical in the brave new world of wine appreciation: How important are grapes?

Here's an idea for you

Try to familiarise yourself with the major grape varieties by always trying to guess which ones are in the wine you are drinking. Initially you'll often get them wrong, but the more you focus on this skill, the more you'll find your way.

To French traditionalists, the origin of a wine is far, far more important than its ingredients – a belief that has much to do with the idea that wine is the product of soil and weather rather than grapes and winemaking. Many French winemakers would also argue that because some of their wines are made from a blend of three or four grapes the finished product is more important than the ingredients.

New World winemakers would beg to differ. For them, wine should be a shining example of the grape it was made from. Chardonnay should conform to the classic fruit and oak combination. Sauvignon Blanc should be fresh and zingy. Cabernet should be deep and berryish. Merlot should be soft and velvety. This, they believe, not only focuses the attention of the winemaker but also simplifies matters by offering the market recognisable names with a range of flavours and aromas that are easy to identify.

Although these two views appear to be contradictory, they aren't necessarily mutually exclusive. There are some wines that express the place where they were made and others that express the grape they were made from.

11. Winemaking 101

If only wine consisted of nothing more than the fermented juice of grapes! In fact, there's a great deal of intervention in the winery, some good, some rather distasteful.

Much of what happens to grapes – particularly those used to make cheap wines – involves compensating for poor-quality grapes. If all grapes were grown in ideal conditions, there would be little need to do much more than crush them and then ferment the juice that remains and for very expensive wines, that is more or less what happens.

For mass-produced wines, the reality is rather different. In order to maximise the quantity of grapes produced, quality falls by the wayside – with the result that people in white coats are required to do their best to compensate. Gleaming, state-of-the-art temperature-controlled equipment

Here's an idea for you

If you really want to understand the difference between wines that are made with painstaking care and those that are made in industrial conditions, simply taste them side by side. Try drinking the most basic Australian Shiraz you can find next to an expensive Syrah from Hermitage in the Rhône Valley and the flavours will talk far more elegantly than any technical guide to winemaking.

helps too, as does the practice of blending grapes of different varieties or grown in different areas in order to iron out imperfections. The leaps and bounds in technology are making the winemakers adept at making silk purses out of sows' ears, so that cheap wine tastes better now than ever before.

Tasting wine won't help you learn much about the winemaking process but it will give you an insight into the effect that it has. Try tasting: some grape juice, very oaky expensive Chardonnay and very cheap Australian Chardonnay. Grape juice is wine that hasn't been fermented, aged in oak or generally messed around with, so it provides a useful comparison to gauge the impact that the winemaking process has had on the other wines. The two other wines give you an opportunity to compare wine that has and hasn't been oaked.

Be aware that the depths of knowledge that can be plumbed are almost fathomless, but ask yourself whether immersing yourself in all this knowledge will really help to deepen your understanding of wine – or whether indeed it might detract from the only two features of any wine that really matter: its flavour and aroma.

12. Oaky, OK?

Of all the flavours in wine, oak is the most easily identified. Here's a guide to spotting it.

Although the use of oak barrels is no longer essential in the winemaking process, it is considered a useful means of enhancing and manipulating the flavour of wine. For makers of inexpensive, mass-market wines, there is a problem in the fact that oak barrels are hugely expensive. For many winemakers, the answer is to treat their wines with what look like giant teabags full of wooden chips that impart the flavour of oak without the expense of oak barrels.

How much does it matter whether a wine derives its oakiness from oak chips or real oak barrels? Not much at all. As the free-thinking drinker that you're becoming, you will appreciate that the most important feature of any wine is not how it was made but its taste and aroma.

Here's an idea for you

Whenever you try a wine, try to determine whether it has been oaked – and, if it has, how successfully it has been done. With time you'll discover the amount of oakiness you like in a wine.

39

You'll find the flavour of oak in both red and white wines. To explore the subject it makes sense to focus on just one grape variety. Try the following wines side by side: unoaked Chardonnay; medium-priced oaky Australian, Californian or South African Chardonnay; oaked Burgundian Chardonnay; and expensive oaked Californian Chardonnay. It is often suggested that oaky wines make good partners to food, so you might like to try these wines with a meal. A wine that might taste overbearingly oaky on its own will seem completely different when it is drunk with grilled chicken. There are many foods – particularly those with very strong flavours – that will make an oaky wine seem considerably less oaky.

Just tasting your way around these wines will quickly give you a handle on the different effects that oak can have on a wine. For most people oak is simply a question of personal taste – like Marmite and Wagner. The truth is that there are good oaky wines and bad oaky wines in equal measure. But, used well, oak is to wine what seasoning is to food – and with all matters of taste it is essential to keep an open mind.

13. Rain or shine

One of the reasons that grapes produce wines with a huge range of different flavours and aromas is that grapes are enormously sensitive to the climate they are grown in.

A grape is no different from any other type of fruit. Bite into an eating apple in early summer when it is still small and green and it will taste wincingly sour. By autumn the same apple will have been exposed to plenty of sun and become sweet and juicy. Grapes follow exactly the same pattern. Those grown in different parts of the world are exposed to greater or lesser amounts of sun and so will display very different characteristics.

Champagne is a good example of wine made from grapes that are the product of a cool northern climate. Because the grapes are never exposed to enough sun to make them fat, ripe and juicy, they make wines that are typically quite sour in character because of their much greater acidity. When the same

Here's an idea for you

When tasting wine blind, try to guess whether it is from the northern or southern hemisphere before revealing its identity.

Defining idea

'There is no such thing as bad weather, only different kinds of good weather.'
JOHN RUSKIN

grapes grown further south are used to make wine, the wines are fruitier because they have been exposed to a greater amount of sunlight.

Taste Test
■ Inexpensive white Burgundy + fruity Australian Chardonnay
■ Inexpensive red Bordeaux + fruity Australian Cabernet

When comparing each of these pairs of wine, try to picture vineyards in Burgundy and Bordeaux that for many months of the year are as sodden and overcast as any other region in northern lands. Next cast your mind several thousand miles southeast to the sun-baked earth of Australia and consider how the warmer climate might have affected the flavour of the grapes.

Warmer temperatures in places such as Australia, Chile and South Africa produce wines that are fruitier and more approachable than those made in Europe's chillier climes. Old-school wine buffs will argue that these New World wines lack such elusive qualities as 'finesse' and 'complexity'. The more you taste, the clearer it will become that the difference between the wines made in these two different climates is not one of quality – it simply concerns their character. And as the free-thinking drinker that you're now becoming you will realise that it pays to keep an open mind.

14. Ageing gracefully

Does all wine improve with age? If not, which wines do? Take your palate on a journey into the past.

The flavour of many wines is intimately related to two key factors: the year it was made in and how long ago it was made. These two factors are inextricably linked. When wine buffs discuss the year – or 'vintage' – of a wine, they are referring to the weather conditions in the year it was made and the impact these might have had on the wine. But as the wine gets older they will also be referring to the way that it is ageing.

In the northern regions, where the climate changes dramatically from one year to the next, wine is more likely to reflect the year in which it was made. In the southern regions, where the weather tends to be less temperamental, wine is more likely to be pretty much the same from year to year.

Here's an idea for you

Almost everyone has old bottles of wine lurking in cupboards. Once you've established that a bottle isn't worth hundred of pounds open it. Even if it's a wine that wasn't made for ageing, it will help you to understand the way that the character of a wine changes over the years.

Defining idea

'Appreciating old wine is like making love to a very old lady. It is possible. It can even be enjoyable. But it requires a bit of imagination.'
ANDRE TCHELISTCHEFF

But even in Europe leaps and bounds in winemaking technology are enabling producers to iron out the effects that a poor harvest might have on a wine. The truth is that the vintage only tends to be of vital importance when you're buying good-quality wines from areas such as Bordeaux and Burgundy.

The vast majority of wines – particularly whites – become increasingly dull and flaccid with age. Only very good-quality red wines, a few whites and some Champagnes become softer and more attractive with age – and even that is very much a matter of personal taste. All other wines are made to be consumed in a year or two.

Taste Test

Old red Bordeaux is expensive, but for the purposes of this Taste Test you can keep costs down by choosing a wine that isn't from one of the star years.

- Cheap one- or two-year-old Cabernet-based red Bordeaux
- Ten-year-old Cabernet-based Bordeaux from a good vintage

15. Words fail me

Most of us find it difficult enough to describe a thought in our heads, let alone the contents of our glass.

The first rule in talking and writing about wine is to try to avoid lengthy fanciful descriptions. Remember that wine appreciation is a wholly subjective field that is as open to interpretation as art or music. One wine lover's 'gnat's pee' is another's 'delightful hedgerow aromas'. So it is essential to develop a personal vocabulary of your own rather than attempt to adopt someone else's.

In your attempts to become more articulate about the contents of your wine glass it is a good idea to write notes using your own descriptions. What do the taste and smell of the wine remind you of? Compare the smell of a glass of Sauvignon Blanc, Pinot Noir or Chardonnay to some other familiar smell and its taste to a familiar flavour. Often the most

Here's an idea for you

Wherever you go carry a notebook in which to write notes on the wine that you drink. You'll probably feel self-conscious about this at first, but friends and colleagues will soon get used to it.

47

meaningful descriptions aren't those that allude to some other flavour or aroma – sometimes they are as simple as 'great length' or 'tightly structured' – but, while I know what they mean, you may not, which is the reason it is essential to develop your own code.

Focus on three key points: colour, flavour and aroma. Try to get into the habit of commenting on all three of these aspects of a wine – even if one or other of them isn't especially noteworthy. When describing flavour, comparisons with fruits are popular, from the humble plum to the exotic lychee. But don't limit yourself to these. What about familiar flavours such as chocolate or liquorice? Comparisons with flowers are useful when describing aromatic wines. But also think laterally. What about tobacco, woodsmoke or cedar? Note the intensity of the wine's colour. Is it light, pallid or opaque? What's important is that they provide a useful shorthand to create a gastronomic word picture. Wine appreciation is an extremely subjective field, so your views are as valid as anyone else's.

16. Cabernet

Cabernet Sauvignon, like Chardonnay, is a wine about which it is virtually impossible to make any sweeping generalisations.

What many Cabernets tend to do, however, is make wines with an attractive three-dimensional quality that are approachable when young – and in some cases sufficiently robust to age beautifully. For these reasons Cabernet is often used in blended wines, either with Merlot or to give body to wines such as Chianti. The grape is the mainstay of many red Bordeaux, particularly those from areas such as the hallowed Medoc. Now the grape is as ubiquitous as Chardonnay, making fabulous long-lived wines everywhere from Bordeaux to the Barossa.

One of the reasons for the success of Australian and Chilean wines, particularly Cabernet, is that winemakers in these countries have succeeded in giving them a dose of sometimes imperceptible sweetness that makes them more approachable than those from

Here's an idea for you

You might like to try comparing these wines with a Merlot, Shiraz, Pinot Noir or red Rioja. The more you try the better because doing so will highlight not just the differences but also the similarities. Each new comparison will help you to build up a crystal-clear profile in your mind of Cabernet's place in the vinous world.

Cabernet's spiritual home in Bordeaux. Like oakiness, sweetness is one of those qualities that is perfectly palatable in a wine when it is balanced with some other pronounced flavour such as acidity.

Cabernet has an affinity with a wide variety of different foods. From a classic combination like mature Cabernet-based red Bordeaux with roast lamb to juicy New World Cabernet with grilled meats, it is a gregarious mixer.

Taste Test
- Expensive Cabernet-based Bordeaux that is no less than five years old
- Inexpensive Chilean Cabernet
- Bulgarian Cabernet
- Californian Cabernet
- Inexpensive Cabernet-based South African blend

Consider the colour, aroma, flavour, whether some of the wines were sweeter than others, and how the wines that include only Cabernet compare with those in which Cabernet has been blended with another grape variety. Think about how each wine would go with food. Would you prefer to drink them on their own? If you would prefer to drink them with food, what kind of food do you think that they would go well with?

17. French classics

How to enjoy classic French wines – and avoid those that are a triumph of flummery over flavour.

Regardless of their quality, many wines from Bordeaux, Burgundy and Champagne sell for two or three times the price of wines from elsewhere that are arguably much better. In order to defend yourself against exploitation you need to know a few facts:

1. Inexpensive Bordeaux, Burgundy or Champagne is almost certain to be pretty grim (unless it's stolen). Your money would almost certainly be much better spent in southern France, Germany, Italy or the New World.

2. It is possible to find delicious, affordable wines from Bordeaux, Burgundy and Champagne, but it requires a great deal of work – which will be more than repaid with wonderful, subtle flavours that are hard to find elsewhere.

3. Good-quality Champagne is one of the world's best-value wines – even when it costs as much as a decent pair of shoes.

Here's an idea for you

Many specialist wine merchants hold fine wine dinners that although quite expensive do allow you to taste a variety of well-chosen, good-quality wines at one sitting. Why not give one a whirl?

Defining idea

'Fame and wealth – all that is illusion.
All that endures is character.'
O. J. SIMPSON

The cost of a tasting that would help you explore the subtleties of the finest Bordeaux, Burgundy and Champagne would be prohibitive. Instead you should treat the matter as a lifetime's journey. Bordeaux alone has almost a quarter of a million acres of vineyard and almost 13,000 producers, so it could take you a lifetime just to get to grips with the wines of this region, let alone those from Burgundy and Champagne.

The good news is that Bordeaux, Burgundy and Champagne by no means have a monopoly on the qualities with which they are traditionally associated. The wonderfully fragile, raspberryish character of fine Burgundy and the cedary aromas of red Bordeaux can now also be found in wines from elsewhere, notably Spain, California and New Zealand. The one exception is Champagne: though sparkling wines from areas such as the Loire, northern Italy and Australia tend to be infinitely better quality than cheap Champagne, it is rare to taste examples that come close to the complexity and wonderful bready aromas of top-notch Champagne.

18. The beautiful south

A hitchhiker's guide to the deep, inky reds and three-dimensional whites of southern France.

Southern France is home to thousands of producers making a multitude of different styles of wine. Although the familiar Chardonnay, Sauvignon, Cabernet and Merlot grapes do grow in the South of France what makes the region's wines so compelling is a host of other grapes such as Carignan, Cinsaut, Mourverde, Grenache, Rolle, Roussanne and Marsanne. These rarely make a solo appearance in wine. Instead they are used in diverse combinations to make blends. Though this fact might make the area seem daunting to wine lovers weaned on single-variety wines, it also helps to make the region's wines so beguiling.

Another attraction of the South of France is that it is almost the antithesis of the corporate, marketing-obsessed wine industries to be found in Australia, California

Here's an idea for you

Find a map that covers the South of France in detail. Whenever you taste a wine from the region try to find the place where it was made. Soon you'll have a clear picture of the complex geography of the region.

and Chile. Many of its best winemakers are small producers scratching a living by making handmade wines with love and care. If you are looking for romance in wine, then you will find it here.

Leave all your preconceptions at the door and search the region's highways and byways for new flavours and aromas. Yes, you might often be disappointed, but for every dull wine you taste you'll find half a dozen winners. So vast is the number of different wines – and the variety of styles – that even a blind tasting of a hundred wines would hardly scratch the surface. What is essential is to try to put the wines in context. How does one of the wonderful reds from an area such as Costieres de Nimes, made from a hotchpotch of grapes such as Grenache Noir, Syrah, Carignan, Mourverde and Cinsaut, compare with a Chilean or South African equivalent made from just one – say, Cabernet, Merlot or Shiraz? Is it better or worse? Which would you rather drink with food?

Although the South of France might be better known for its reds and rosés, there are also plenty of whites that will revive anyone with a palate that has been worn out by oaky Chardonnays and assertive Sauvignons: vibrant, tangy whites such as Picpoul de Pinet.

19. Lovely bubbly?

Although many people regard fizzy wine as a treat there's no doubt that bubbles can mask some pretty tawdry, hangover-inducing wines.

Fizz – and Champagne in particular – is nothing more than a wine and its success or failure depends not on the bubbles but on the wine used to make it. For proof you simply need to keep a glass of leftover sparkling wine or Champagne in a fridge until it is flat. Stripped of its bubbles what does it taste like when compared with your favourite white? The answers to this question will not only provide an insight into the quality of the wine but also help to deepen your understanding of sparkling wines.

Taste Test
- Expensive vintage Champagne
- Grand Marque Champagne
- Cheap Champagne (the cheapest you can find in a supermarket)
- Mid-price Australian sparkling wine
- Prosecco

Here's an idea for you

Drinking bad Champagne is as instructive as drinking delicious ones. When you taste a bad Champagne don't dismiss it immediately. Struggle on to the end of the glass so that you can identify that it really is bad. The next delicious glass will taste all the more delicious.

Defining idea

'Come quickly, I'm tasting stars.'
DOM PERIGNON, on discovering Champagne

First, serve all the wines together and record your observations, especially on the differences between the various wines. You could also give marks out of ten for flavour and aroma. Take your time on this and remember that what you are tasting is a wine. Don't be distracted by either the bubbles or your preconceptions. Next, reveal the wines' identities and prices and compare them with your marks. It would also be a very useful exercise to put all the wines in the fridge for a couple of days and try them again when they are flat.

Style guide
- Non-vintage. Made from a blend of wines from two or more years. Blending allows the wine to have a consistent style.
- Vintage. A Champagne made from wines from just one very good year. No guarantee of quality, since what constitutes a 'good year' is debatable.
- Blanc de blanc. Champagne made from Chardonnay.
- Blanc de noirs. Champagne made of Pinot Noir and/or Pinot Meunier.
- Rosé. Pink Champagne made from black grapes, or ordinary Champagne coloured with red wine.

20. Spanish highs

Spanish wines still present something of a minefield to the casual buyer, but a casual buyer's minefield is the free-thinking drinker's gold mine.

Start your tour of Spanish wines with a scattergun approach that will help you find the styles you like. Over a period of a couple of weeks taste as many reds as you can from the two areas that are best known for their red wines: Rioja and Ribero del Duero. Having identified your favourite wines from both areas, taste them again alongside other reds that you know well. A good possible line-up could include: Ribera del Duero x 2, Rioja x 2, Chilean Cabernet Sauvignon, a southern French red, Rhône red and a good mature red Bordeaux.

Take a similar approach with the whites. Again, start with Rioja: try a handful of whites before moving on to Galicia, where you should try any Albarinos you can lay your hands on. Finally, select your two favourite wines from each area. For your taste test you might then compare: white

Here's an idea for you

Spain's wine regions are as complex as those in the South of France. As you try the wines, plot their position on a map of Spain. This discipline helps focus the mind and you'll discover all sorts of places that you never knew existed.

Rioja x 2, Albarino x 2, New Zealand Sauvignon, good oaky Australian Chardonnay, Muscadet and Verdicchio.

As in France, the focus of the winemaker is on style rather than grapes – of which there are almost 600 different varieties in Spain. From a filleting perspective the only grapes you need to concern yourself with are Tempranillo, used to makes red wines in Ribera del Duero, and Garnacha – the grape that the French call 'Grenache Noir'. The two white grapes to focus on initially are Albarino and Viura, the grape in white Rioja.

Spanish wines can be classified as either 'typical', which adhere to a style true to the region where they are made, or 'modern', which seek to mimic the styles of wine from the southern hemisphere. There is nothing intrinsically wrong with the latter, but in the interest of deepening your knowledge of Spanish wines it makes sense to avoid them.

21. Using sommeliers

So you find the people who serve wine in restaurants patronising and unnecessary? You clearly haven't read the operating manual...

Whatever your level of knowledge, the advantage of using a sommelier is that they know the wines on their lists like the backs of their hands – from background information about the winery to the intimate details of the vintages. Better still, their art is to suggest which wines will go best with your choice of food. The best sommeliers are those who are able to educate their customers, not by firing reams of information at them but by broadening their vinous horizons with suggestions of wines that they might not otherwise have been brave enough to try.

Don't be afraid of sommeliers. Most are passionate about their subject and keen to share their knowledge. If you are at a restaurant primarily to enjoy the food rather than to do business, their advice is likely to enhance your enjoyment.

Here's an idea for you

The next time you are faced with a sommelier try to give them as wide a brief as possible. Try not to specify the wine that you want, or else at least pitch your request in the form 'red Bordeaux or something similar in style'.

Defining idea

'The wise man is not the man who gives the right answers: he is the one who asks the right questions.'
CLAUDE LEVI-STRAUSS

One of the dangers of some sommeliers is that they may be keen to push expensive wines or those with a high profit margin. Although you might not wish to appear mean by asking the price, do tread with care and if you feel uncertain ask to see the name of the wine and its price before ordering. If the sommelier suggests a wine that you know you don't like, don't be afraid to ask for other suggestions.

If you discover a sommelier you like and trust, try to make that restaurant a regular haunt. The more a sommelier understands your likes and dislikes, the more fruitful will be the relationship.

22. The wizards of Oz

Do Australian winemakers make wines that are fresh, vibrant and fruity or dull, boring and a triumph of marketing? It's time to make up your mind on where you stand on the great Australian wine debate.

The case for Australia: Big, consistent, fruit-driven wines with easy to understand labels.

The case against: Australia produces dull, predictable, fruit-driven wines that are overpriced – in comparison both with other countries in the southern hemisphere where costs are cheaper and also with most European wine regions.

Yes, it's easy to become bored by the rather homogeneous style of Australian wines, but there will also be times when that type of wine is precisely what you want. There is also no doubt that the pioneering spirit of Australian winemakers has made them masters of innovation

Here's an idea for you

You'll gain a better insight into Australian wine if you have a good understanding of the food. Find a book on Australian cookery that will give you a good idea of its big pronounced flavours created with gutsy ingredients such as garlic, apricots, oranges, capers and figs.

who have recently achieved great things with obscure, offbeat grape varieties such as Verdelho and Gewürztraminer that have been unloved and overlooked by others.

Taste Test – reds
- Good-quality Coonawarra Cabernet + good-quality red Bordeaux
- Good-quality Barossa Shiraz + good-quality Rhône red

Taste Test – whites
- Hunter Valley Chardonnay + good white Burgundy
- Clare Valley Riesling + German Riesling
- Good-quality Semillon + Semillon-based white Bordeaux
- Western Australian Sauvignon + Loire Sauvignon

You will have noticed that I have suggested for the Taste Test wines that come from specific areas. As the Australian wine industry has grown ever more sophisticated, winemakers are learning more about which grapes respond best to which areas. The result is that there is a new emphasis on regionality. The more you explore Australian wines, the more you'll discover these regional differences. The more you learn, the more you'll realise that anyone who makes generalisations about Australian wines is sure to be a bluffer.

Defining idea

'In a climate so favourable, the cultivation of vines may doubtless be carried to a degree of perfection.'
CAPTAIN ARTHUR PHILLIP, commander of the fleet that carried the first British settlers to Sydney in 1788

23. Cork talk

Once you know how, spotting corked wine is easy – but the fact is that you shouldn't have to.

It takes time to learn to distinguish different characters in a wine – and corkiness is one of them. The mistake of confusing corkiness with oakiness, for example, isn't the heinous crime that it might seem. It isn't until you've tasted a half a dozen corked wines that their smell becomes so distinct.

There are a variety of different euphemisms for corkiness. One of the most common is 'musty', which isn't especially helpful because there are some wines – expensive red Rhônes, for example – that have that trait. A more useful comparison is wet cardboard. Because corkiness is more evident in the aroma of a wine than in the flavour, most wine buffs simply need to sniff a wine to tell whether it is corked. It is for this reason that trying the wine is more than just a ritual.

Here's an idea for you

Identifying the smell of wet cardboard will help you to sniff out corkiness. The best way to do this is to soak some cardboard in water overnight and put the pulp in a glass – breathe deeply and you will have a pretty good idea of what you are looking for.

If you have an agreeable wine merchant or a friend who is knowledgeable about wine, ask them to save the next bottle of badly corked wine they come across so you can test it against another bottle of the same wine in good condition. The glaring difference should imprint itself on your mind so indelibly that you couldn't fail to spot a corked wine in future.

However, there's no longer any reason why white wines and everyday reds should ever be afflicted in this way. With the exception of high-quality reds intended for ageing, which do benefit from their corks, all other wines should be fitted with metal screw caps that can simply be twisted off. Not only do such caps solve the problem of wines becoming corked, they also keep the wine fresher and more vibrant. The only reason that screw caps haven't caught on more quickly is prejudice – they are still associated for many people with cheap wines. Moreover, many drinkers prefer the ritual of pulling a cork rather than the less romantic business of twisting a metal cap.

24. Fantasy island

Thirty years ago the idea that New Zealand would one day become a source of some of the world's best-quality red and white wines would have been treated with a loud guffaw among wine buffs.

New Zealand has succeeded more than any other New World region in beating the French at their own game. While Loire producers complacently churned out Sauvignon Blancs that relied more on their name than their flavour, the New Zealanders set about making their own Sauvignons that delivered punchy, vibrant freshness almost eye-watering in its intensity.

Over the last decade or so, new grapes and styles have proliferated. But what has been the secret of New Zealand's success? A key factor has been climate. You only need to look at photographs of the lush, misty landscape of areas such as Marlborough, New Zealand's most successful winemaking region, to

Here's an idea for you

Try tasting a Sauvignon from New Zealand and another from the Loire (blind) with a fish dish. The chances are that they will respond to food in very different ways.

realise that such country offers the perfect conditions for crisp, cool-climate wines of the kind previously associated with areas such as the Loire, Burgundy, Germany and Alsace.

Taste Test
• Good-quality New Zealand Sauvignon Blanc • New Zealand Riesling • New Zealand Pinot Gris • Sancerre or Pouilly Fume • Pinot Grigio • Dry-style German Riesling • Burgundian Pinot Noir.

Carry out random comparisons before trying out the following combinations:
■ New Zealand Sauvignon Blanc + Pouilly Fume or Sancerre
■ New Zealand Riesling + dry-style German Riesling
■ New Zealand Pinot Gris + Pinot Grigio
■ New Zealand Pinot Noir + Burgundian Pinot Noir

If you detected a difference in style between the wines in the taste test this is a good time to think about the different approaches to winemaking in different wine regions. There is a tendency among New World winemakers – particularly those in New Zealand – to extract every last drop of flavour out of a grape whereas those in Europe tend to go for wines with a little more subtlety. Those who champion the cause of New World winemakers might say that their in-your-face wines are simply the result of superior winemaking skills.

25. California dreaming

Like any wine region, California evades generalisations. As you will discover, it's the home of good and boring wines in equal measure.

One problem that has blighted the Californian wine industry in recent years has been the fierce competition generated by the arrival of good-value wines from Chile and Australia. In addition the exponential growth in the number of wineries has created such a serious glut that Californian producers have had to drop prices in order to remain competitive. Good news for drinkers: oversupply means good-value wines – in many cases superb examples of their type.

California's speciality grape is Zinfandel, a grape of obscure origins that makes wonderfully bold reds and terrible rosé known as 'blush'. Vines have been grown in the region since the 1770s, but it wasn't until the gold rush in the 1850s that an influx of thirsty prospectors created a market for locally produced wines. It wasn't until the 1960s that a new generation of dry table wines – notably Cabernet Sauvignon and

Here's an idea for you

As food and wine matching is such an intrinsic part of the region's gastronomic heritage, it makes sense to match Californian wines with food, preferably with sunny Californian-style food.

67

Defining idea

'The great majority of those who speak of perfectibility as a dream, do so because they feel that it is one which would afford them no pleasure if it is realised.'
JOHN STUART MILL

Chardonnay – gained serious recognition, notably at a landmark tasting in 1976 when some Californian reds beat classed growth chateaux in a blind tasting.

Taste Test – whites

• Californian Chardonnay • Good-quality Australian Chardonnay • Good Californian sparkling wine • Good Champagne • Australian sparkling wine

Taste Test – reds

• Californian Cabernet • Australian Cabernet • Red Bordeaux • Californian Zinfandel • Californian Pinot Noir • Good-quality Burgundy • Australian Cabernet Sauvignon • Good-quality Cabernet-based red Bordeaux • Rhône red

Having tried the wines blind, try the following line-up:

■ Californian Chardonnay + good-quality Californian Chardonnay
■ Californian Cabernet + Australian Cabernet + Cabernet-based red Bordeaux
■ Californian Zinfandel + Rhône red + Californian Cabernet
■ Californian Pinot Noir + good-quality Burgundy
■ Good Californian sparkling wine + good Champagne + Australian sparkling wine

26. Italian renaissance

Modern Italian producers are creating wines that offer light relief from the predictable flavours of Aussie Chardonnay.

Fans of Italian wine love the quirks and eccentricities to be found in the character reds and quirky whites of Tuscany, Piedmont, the Veneto, Basilicata and Sicily. There is also no doubt, too, that many people are attracted by the romance of Italian wine – the exquisite castelli, sweeping vineyards, crumbling wineries and fabulous food proving the theory that wine drinkers are better disposed towards wine regions where they would actually like to be. The bad news is that Italy now provides a more complex minefield for drinkers than ever before, with the result that it demands more radical filleting than almost any other wine region.

Taste Test – reds
• Barolo • Good-quality Chianti •
Inexpensive Chianti • Salice
Salentino • Expensive Australian or
Chilean Cabernet

Here's an idea for you

Italians see wine as part of their culture. However corny it might sound, it always helps to create the right environment in which to enjoy Italian wine – with the help of some prosciutto, bread, olive oil. Yes, and some Verdi...

To help your palate feels its way around the different flavours, compare these wines side by side so that you get a feel for the profile of the different flavours and aromas offered by each of them.

Taste Test – whites
• Soave • Frascati • Orvieto • Sicilian Chardonnay • Verdicchio dei Castelli di Jesi

Again, taste each of the still wines side by side and then the two sparkling wines.

With a few exceptions these are wines in which style and region take precedence over the grape variety. Chianti, for example, is made from a blend that includes a grape called Sangiovese that is indigenous to Italy, Soave is made from Garganega and Trebbiano del Soave and Barolo from Nebbiolo.

Tasting Italian wines also requires a particular mindset. As in many countries where wine is ingrained into the national gastronomic culture, wine is an integral part of a meal but not the main attraction. Anyone used to the big, attention-grabbing flavours of New World wines will find the more shy and retiring nature of wines such as Soave and Frascati hard to fathom. Imagine drinking them with a spaghetti carbonara on a boiling hot afternoon in Tuscany and their appeal suddenly becomes more apparent.

27. Sherry baby

A sickly old-fashioned drink fit only for the plughole, or one of the world's best-value and underrated drinks? Focus your attention on Fino and you might soon have an opinion.

The reason for the huge success of Sherry during the 50s and 60s was that it was an inexpensive, potent and supposedly long-lived alternative to wine. Now that wine is cheaper we think nothing of cracking open a bottle at the drop of a hat. But Fino Sherry is arguably the most delicious, best-value, highest-quality wine known to humankind. In order to decide where you stand on the issue you need to undertake a most dramatic exercise in filleting: *imagine that the only style of Sherry in existence is Fino.*

Sounds radical, but like all the filleting suggestions, the idea is not that you never allow any other type of Sherry to pass your lips, but simply that if you are to learn to understand Fino you must renounce all other Sherries.

Here's an idea for you

Keep a bottle of Sherry in the fridge for use as an early evening sharpener. One evening you could even try drinking it as an accompaniment to food. Just remember that it has quite a high alcohol content.

Sherry is made in Andalucia near the seaside towns of Jerez de la Frontera ('Jerez' is the origin of the English name 'Sherry'), Sanlucar de Barrameda and Puerto de Santa Maria. The Palomino Fino grape used makes pretty dull table wines but great Fino Sherry thanks to a natural yeast called 'flor' that is created by the Sherry-making process. Fino is created by a curious, complex process known as the solera system in which after a few years in the barrel a third of the oldest Sherry is bottled and the remainder is topped up with younger Sherry before being aged further.

Taste Test
• Good-quality Fino • Cheap Fino • Cheap Port • Pouilly Fume • White Rioja • Cheap Australian Chardonnay.

Tasting these wines side by side will help you to put the unique character of Fino into context. The point to remember when tasting these wines is that unlike the others (with the exception of the Port) Fino is fortified to a strength of around 15% – double that of some light German wines and a third more than most white wines. On an empty stomach you'll find that it packs an even more powerful punch.

28. Que Syrah, Syrah

Cabernet might be the ubiquitous crowd pleaser but Syrah is the variety that has succeeded in beguiling winemakers all over the world from the Rhône Valley to Australia's Barossa Valley.

In the Rhône, where Syrah is used to make legendary long-lived red wines such as Hermitage, the grape is known as 'Syrah'. In Australia and South Africa the grape is known is known as 'Shiraz'. The difference isn't just one of name: in different climates, Syrah/Shiraz is used to produce two entirely different styles of wine. In the Rhône, Syrah is either used on its own or blended with a variety of other reds such as Cinsault Carignan and Mourverdre. In the New World, particularly in Australia, the grape is used on its own or sometimes blended with Cabernet.

Of all its different Rhône guises, the most legendary is as the ruinously expensive, long-lived Hermitage. The grape is thought to have been exported to Australia by James Busby, the father of Australian

Here's an idea for you

The Rhône is another wine region that needs a map. Start putting all the famous names such as Hermitage and Chateauneuf du Pape into context by studying a good map as you taste the wines.

viticulture. A century later it gained a legendary reputation as Grange, a fabulously complex red made in the Barossa by Max Schubert, the chief winemaker at Penfolds. The wine, which doesn't show its best qualities until after a decade or so, is widely acknowledged as one of Australia's greatest wines and proved to sniffy Europeans that Australian winemakers could make serious wine.

The difference between Shiraz and Syrah will become clear in the following Taste Test:
- Red Hermitage or Crozes Hermitage (entirely Syrah based)
- Rhône red made from a blend of grapes including Syrah
- Inexpensive Australian Shiraz
- Expensive Barossa Shiraz
- South African Shiraz
- Good-quality Australian Cabernet

How do those produced in the hotter climate of Australia compare with those produced in the Rhône? Are there any differences between the South African and the Australian Shiraz?

Australian Shiraz is one of those wines sometimes described as a 'food wine'. The term is a euphemism for a wine that would taste much too overpowering on its own and needs to be tempered by the soothing effects of food.

29. The merchants of menace

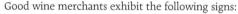

Forget the stereotypes: the joy of wine merchants is that they are knowledgeable enthusiasts who love their subject. Not something that you'll ever find in a supermarket.

Good wine merchants exhibit the following signs:

- They offer you a chance to try wines.
- They don't sell cigarettes and sweets by the till.
- They sell specialist wine magazines, fancy corkscrews and wine glasses.

In order to use a wine merchant successfully you need a tactical, focused approach. Be specific and set parameters, particularly when looking for wines to be used in a Taste Test. A good approach might be 'Please could I have a good-value New Zealand Sauvignon Blanc' or 'Do you have a good-quality, typical Sancerre?'.

Here's an idea for you

Try to identify a local wine merchant that has a member of staff in whom you have confidence – by asking a few questions and trying out his or her recommendations. An ongoing relationship is more fruitful than occasional encounters, since you will begin to understand one another's likes and dislikes.

A wine merchant can be a good source of advice – but remember that the key to achieving vinous nirvana is not to let yourself become a receptacle for other people's opinions. Also remember that wine merchants are salespeople. So beware: they might have a reason to sell you one wine rather than another – such as the fact that it has a higher profit margin or it needs to be shifted. Question everything they tell you. And if you like wines they have recommended, tell them. Handled carefully, merchants can be guides who will offer essential advice to the free-thinking drinker.

This is where wine merchants really come into their own. Although supermarkets are undoubtedly a great source of good-value branded wines, their wine, like anything else on the supermarket shelves, is more a matter of profit margins than quality. On the whole, supermarkets favour fast-selling wines that are supplied in large quantities rather than offbeat wines that don't make a quick, profitable return. Though wine merchants also need to make a profit from their wines, they are aware that their raison d'être is to offer greater choice to a more discerning audience.

30. The perfect match

The art of matching food and wine has spawned countless rules and regulations dreamt up by obsessive foodies. However, the key to a sensual, satisfying relationship is an open mind.

It is essential that you make your own journey when exploring which food goes well with which wine. Try the following combinations:

- Hot spicy lamb curry + New Zealand Sauvignon Blanc + Australian Shiraz
- Chicken in tarragon sauce + New Zealand Sauvignon Blanc + Australian Shiraz + oaky Australian Chardonnay

How did the flavours of the wines respond to the different types of food, and vice versa? The secret of a good wine match is very much like the secret of a good wine: it is essential to achieve a good balance of flavours. Better still, a

Here's an idea for you

Always try to keep two to three bottle of wine open at any given time. The more combinations you try, the greater chance you'll have of finding a good match.

Defining idea

combination of complementary flavours can make for a heavenly combination. One sensible approach to the business of food and wine matching is to try – whenever possible – to combine food that is typical of a region with its wines, e.g. red Burgundy with boeuf bourguignon, Swiss whites with fondue, Moroccan reds with tagine.

When you start investigating wine in the context of food and food in the context of wine, you're pulling the lid off a vast arena of gastronomy. Matching food and wine is not a subject that can be easily regulated. For years there was a fervently held belief that cheese should only ever be taken with red wines and sweet wines until one esteemed wine expert was brave enough to stick his hand up and say he felt that soft, creamy cheeses with delicate flavours were far better suited to white wines than reds.

The only golden rule is not about which wine you should drink with which food but says that you should treat wine as an intrinsic part of the gastronomic experience. Wine doesn't exist to be tasted in the clinical environment of a tasting room with nothing more than a dry biscuit for company. Almost all wine (however bad) tastes better with food than without it.

31. Money talks

The joy of being a free-thinking drinker is that you'll be able to spot a rip-off wine at fifty paces.

When you look at the price of a family car it is completely apparent why one model is more expensive than another. When you look at a wine list the reason that one wine is twice the price of another is far from obvious.

Why some wines are cheap

- They are made in countries where land and labour are cheap, e.g. South America and Eastern Europe.
- They are made from grapes grown in hot regions where vines are irrigated in order to produce a large quantity of fruit that lacks flavour – a problem solved in the winery by the use of additives such as oak chips.
- They are made in an area where there happens to be huge oversupply.
- They are made by large producers able to take advantage of economies of scale.

Here's an idea for you

When conducting taste tests try to guess the approximate price of the wine in your glass. Doing so will focus your mind on the correlation between price and quality – or, indeed, the lack of it.

- They are on special offer – usually an occasional discount that is almost always funded by desperate producers in order to secure a permanent listing with a retailer.
- They don't taste very nice.

Why some wines are expensive
- They are made in countries where land and labour are expensive.
- They come from a region or producer that has traditionally been held in high esteem, e.g. Bordeaux, Burgundy and Champagne.
- They are painstakingly made by small specialist producers that are unable to take advantage of economies of scale.
- They are made from a particularly good vintage (a point most relevant to Bordeaux, Burgundy and Champagne).
- They are promoted with expensive marketing campaigns.
- They taste delicious.

As you can see, there are plenty of reasons why wines can be cheap or expensive that don't necessarily have anything to do with their quality. It is because wine is such a subjective field that some producers are able to charge high prices for very ordinary wines. The corollary is that wines produced in regions where land and labour are expensive have to do a great deal to convince the world that they have some sort of divinely ordained mystique.

32. In the mix

Many of the world's greatest wines are made from a blend of different grapes. It's time to decide whether you like your grapes straight or mixed.

A huge number of European wines – and an increasing number of New World wines – are made from blends. Most red Bordeaux is made from a blend, as are southern French reds and Champagne – not to mention a host of Spanish and Italian wines that have for years been made from a number of different grapes.

Blending is a hugely complex art that involves using the different components to create just the right style. It's a skill not dissimilar to mixing paint colours to create precisely the right hue – and almost as difficult.

Try the following line-up: inexpensive Australian or Chilean Cabernet + New Zealand Pinot Noir + southern French blend + red Bordeaux blend

Here's an idea for you

To help you understand how different flavours combine together, focus on the taste of all the composite ingredients in a cocktail such as a Bloody Mary to see how different flavours react with one another.

Before you reveal the identity of the wines see if you can tell which of them is made from just one grape and which are blended. Once you know what they are, compare the flavours and aromas of the blended and unblended wines.

White wines tend to be blended less frequently than reds, but there are an increasing number of delicious examples, including successful blends of Chardonnay and Sauvignon Blanc that demonstrate the best of each grape's qualities. Perhaps the best-known example of a blended white is Champagne, which may be made of blends of Chardonnay, Pinot Noir and Pinot Meunier.

Sometimes when winemakers blend wines they are compensating for the failings of one wine with the strengths of another. Another weapon in the blender's armoury is blending not just wines made from different grapes but also wines from different regions and vintages to create a wine that is hopefully much better than the sum of its parts.

Though the modernists are naturally drawn to the simplicity of the idea of wines made from just one grape, even winemakers in the world's most progressive wine regions are discovering the joys of blending, particularly with Bordeaux and Rhône blends. The fact is that there isn't a right or a wrong approach. Some wines lend themselves to blending; others are better suited to a solo performance.

33. On doctor's orders?

The wine industry might try to promote wine as an intrinsic part of a healthy diet, but there is no doubt that the effects of heavy drinking are calamitous.

However much the pro-wine lobby might champion the cause of wine consumption, wine is known to be linked to liver damage, brain damage, cancer, nerve and muscle wasting, blood disorders, raised blood pressure, strokes, skin infections, psoriasis, infertility and birth defects. Wine consumption can also be blamed for all sorts of collateral damage such as road accidents and domestic violence.

Yet, aside from the rash claims made by studies published by various universities (many of which happen to be located in winemaking regions such as Bordeaux and Burgundy), there is fairly convincing evidence that moderate wine consumption does have some benefits. Drinking

Here's an idea for you

Try to follow the French habit of only ever drinking wine with a meal. Not only does wine taste better with food; it also means that there is something to soak it up. Also have plenty of water at hand. It never pays to quench your thirst with wine.

between one and three glasses of wine a day is believed to reduce the chances of death from cardiovascular disease. Despite technically being toxic, alcohol offers such benefits as controlling the levels of blood cholesterol and blood-clotting proteins.

One of the great planks of the wine–health debate is based on what is known as the 'French paradox' – the discovery made by US documentary makers that, despite a relatively high intake of alcohol, the French were generally much healthier than people in Anglo-Saxon countries where drinking is more moderate. If this is true, then one of the contributory factors – besides the 'Mediterranean diet', high in fresh fruit and olive oil – might be the rate at which alcohol is consumed. The tendency in many Northern European countries is to binge, i.e. to concentrate drinking into a relatively short period of time. In France, since wine is an intrinsic part of the gastronomic experience, the rule seems to be 'a little but often'.

There is also an argument that those who see wines as a source of aesthetic pleasure are likely to drink less wine than those who drink simply to get drunk. The more that free-thinking drinkers immerse themselves in the field of wine appreciation by learning to savour the wonderful flavours and aromas that wine offers, the less they will see wine as a social prop.

34. Eastern promise

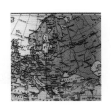

In the eighteenth century Eastern Europe was home to some of the world's greatest wines. Will its star ever rise again?

There is a theory – let's call it the 'Bring Me Sunshine' theory – that drinkers are better disposed towards wines made in sunny countries where they might like to go on holiday than they are towards those from countries that they regard as chilly and, um, a little austere. If this is true, then it might explain the resistance to wines from Eastern Europe.

There was a brief moment back in the 80s when it seemed that the time had come for the wines of Eastern Europe. Bulgarian Cabernet Sauvignon in particular became a common sight on the tables of British wine drinkers. But in the mid 90s Eastern Europe's role as a source of cheap, palatable wines was thwarted by two factors – the lifting of sanctions upon the export of South African wines and

Here's an idea for you

Such is the poor reputation of Eastern European wine that many people reject it out of hand. If you find an example that stands out well in a Taste Test try serving it to people blind. Most drinkers are far more open minded about wine if they can't see the label.

the considerable investment in the Chilean industry – which resulted in lots of competition from a new generation of cheap, cheery wines from the southern hemisphere. There are even those who believe that during the period that economic sanctions were imposed by many countries on South Africa, South African wine was shipped to Eastern Europe, where it was bottled as 'Bulgarian'.

Whatever prejudices you may have about Eastern Europe and its wines, the only way that you can judge them objectively is with blind tasting:

- Bulgarian Cabernet Sauvignon + inexpensive Chilean Cabernet Sauvignon + inexpensive southern French red
- Hungarian Sauvignon Blanc + Chilean Sauvignon Blanc + Hungarian Riesling + inexpensive German Riesling + Italian Pinot Grigio + inexpensive Australian Chardonnay

If you need evidence that Eastern Europe has the potential to make fabulous fine wines, you only have to look back 350 years to the Tokaj-Hegyalja region in the northeast of Hungary. Soon Tokaji (or 'Tokay' as it is known in English-speaking countries) was one of Europe's most sought-after wines, famed for its delicate sweetness and enjoyed by the Russian and French courts as well as the Hapsburgs. It remains one of the world's most delicious wines.

35. Port

Is Port little more than a guaranteed path to a hangover? Or is it one of the world's most artfully made wines? You decide.

Like Sauternes and some of Germany's finest wines, Port suffers from the problem associated with all sweet wines: prejudice. But the problem is not one of sweetness but of quality.

Styles of Port

- Vintage Port is made from the best grapes from a particularly good harvest and becomes increasingly mellow with age.
- Tawny Port is aged in oak casks for ten, twenty or thirty years before bottling.
- Colheita is tawny Port from a single vintage.
- Late-bottled vintage Port is aged for four to six years in casks.

Taste Test

Explore the different styles in the cold light of day and you might start to see Port not as a sickly sweet drink that you consume when you are already inebriated

Here's an idea for you

Try combining Port with different foods. Start with classic accompaniments such as almonds or blue cheese and then try rich puddings such as chocolate ones. Alternatively, something as simple as a slice of melon can work wonders.

but simply as yet another style of wine. Line up the following wines: inexpensive Port + late-bottled vintage Port that is at least ten years old + a sweetish style of New World Cabernet + a dry red (e.g. Burgundy) + tawny Port (served slightly chilled)

The main aim is to assess the balance between sweetness and any other flavours you might find. Look too at the relationship between colour and flavour.

Though the people who make Port are enthusiastic drinkers of their own wine, the last thing that anyone would want to sip on a terrace at the end of a hot day in the Douro Valley is a tepid glass of vintage Port. The answer? White Port – a curious wine that is made from white grapes in almost exactly the same way as red Port is made. Mixed with ice and tonic it serves the same purpose as drinks such as Pimm's: a cool, refreshing drink with a wonderfully tangy, palate-enlivening flavour.

36. Brave New World

The term 'New World' is really a shorthand and refers more to the different climates and philosophies that distinguish New World wines from those made in the Old World.

Wine has been made in many 'New World' regions for hundreds of years. An early Dutch governor of South Africa, Simon van der Stel, established a vineyard in that country way back in 1685, wine has been made in Australia since the early nineteenth century and in California winemaking flourished to supply the huge number of prospectors drawn to the region by the great Gold Rush of the 1850s.

There are a few notable differences between Old and New World wines:

- New World wines have the name of the grape on the bottle. Old World wines don't.
- New World wines tend to be made from just one grape variety. Old World wines are often made from a blend.

Here's an idea for you

Whenever you try a wine blind, try to identify whether it is from the 'Old World' or the 'New World'. The number of times that you get it wrong might make you decide that these terms no longer have much relevance.

91

Defining idea

'I called the New World into existence to redress the balance of the old.'
GEORGE CANNING, British prime minister

■ New World wines offer plenty of information on the label. Old World wines offer very little.

The two regions also produce different flavours resulting from different climates and exhibit different approaches to winemaking. From the results of the following Taste Test try to define exactly what sets the New World and the Old World apart:

■ Australian Cabernet + aged, Cabernet-based red Bordeaux
■ Chablis + Australian Chardonnay

Because of the success of New World wines many European wine producers have set out to mimic their style. So you'll find wines from regions such as the South of France, Italy and Eastern Europe which are almost identical in style and have similar labels to wines from Australia, Chile and New Zealand.

Hardened fans of Old World wines criticise New World wines as too simple, lacking in character and all tasting the same. Devotees of New World wines believe that 'character' is simply an excuse for sloppy winemaking and that the best wines are those that maximise the flavour and aroma of the grapes. The free-thinking drinker knows that when it comes to wine there are plenty of exceptions to every rule.

37. Fine and dandy

What does 'fine' mean in the context of wine? Is it simply used to justify high prices or is it a genuinely useful term that offers some guarantee of quality?

The term 'everyday wine' is useful shorthand for wine that is of basic quality – simple, attractive and a good all-round companion to food. The quality of everyday wine has improved dramatically in the last twenty years.

'Global everyday wine' is usually made from well-known grape varieties such as Chardonnay and Cabernet and tastes the same wherever it is made. 'Country-specific everyday wine' – most of it made in Europe –reflects the winemaking culture of the region in which it was produced.

Fine wine aims to reflect one or more of the following:

- the climate and soil of the landscape where it was made
- the grape – or grapes – from which it was made
- the year in which it was made.

Here's an idea for you

Try comparing an expensive, prestigious fine wine with a favourite, more offbeat wine from the South of France or Spain. Consider the difference in price and then decide whether or not it's really worth paying for a fancy wine.

Defining idea

'Wine is art. It's culture, it's the essence of civilisation.'
ROBERT MONDAVI, Californian winemaker

In order to achieve any one of these things it is essential that the wine is made with care and from the highest-quality grapes. A fine wine won't necessarily offer more sensual enjoyment than an everyday wine. Tasting it might be more of an intellectual challenge, but it won't necessarily be as enjoyable as a simple bottle of plonk drunk with a steak.

This Taste Test includes examples of fine wines, global wines and country-specific everyday wines. Try marking the wines when you are tasting them blind so that you can compare them with their prices: expensive red Bordeaux from a vintage in the early 90s + expensive Australian Shiraz + inexpensive Chilean Merlot + inexpensive but attractive Valpolicella

You might discover wines that are technically 'fine' but which you don't find especially attractive – particularly among those from Australia.

Don't allow yourself to be conned into thinking that all fine wines have fancy names and fancy prices. Though you will pay a premium for wines from a prestigious producer, it is quite possible to find beautifully crafted wines in more offbeat regions such as the South of France and Spain.

38. Simply reds

Once you've mastered Cabernet Sauvignon, Merlot, Shiraz and Pinot Noir, get your head round the flavours that Malbec, Cabernet Franc, Pinotage, Zinfandel and Carmenere have to offer.

Discovering new flavours and aromas is an essential part of wine appreciation. The reason that a relatively small number of grapes have achieved such a monopoly over our palate is that they are tried and tested. The longer that winemakers work with them, the deeper their knowledge becomes and the greater the opportunities they have to exploit these grapes to their full potential. What is more exciting is when little-known grapes come to the fore and are used to create previously unknown flavours and aromas.

Offbeat red grapes

- Cabernet Franc. Often seen as Cabernet Sauvignon's poor relation, this grape makes wonderful wine in the Loire and increasingly in Australia, South America and California.

Here's an idea for you

As well as comparing these offbeat wines, try matching them to a variety of different foods. You'll be amazed at the successful pairings you'll discover.

- Carmenere. Enjoying a revival, particularly in Chile, where it produces big, structured wines not dissimilar in style to Cabernet. It is thought to have originated in Bordeaux.
- Malbec. Another French grape variety that is enjoying a renaissance in South America. In southwest France it is the key ingredient in wines such as Cahors, but in Chile and Argentina it creates wonderfully lush wines that make good alternatives to red Bordeaux.
- Pinotage. A real Frankenstein grape created in South Africa in the 20s by crossing Pinot Noir with Cinsault. It is making wonderful robust reds of increasing sophistication.
- Zinfandel. A robust grape variety that the Californians have made their own.

Taste Test

Argentinian Cabernet Franc + Chilean Malbec + South African Pinotage + Californian Zinfandel + Chilean Carmenere

To put these wines in context, compare them with a Cabernet Sauvignon that you know very well. As you will have discovered, there's a great deal more to red wine than you thought. The reason the wines are so different is not just the different climate but also the pioneering spirit of winemakers in countries like Australia, Chile and California. In many cases New World winemakers are teaching those in the Old World about the unexploited potential of grapes that they had previously overlooked.

39. Hot off the marks

Australia, New Zealand and California might have had a head start in the race to create fabulous, world-class wines but South Africa and Chile aren't far behind.

Despite its centuries-old history, winemaking in South Africa didn't fulfil its potential until the 90s, when the first free elections precipitated closer ties with the rest of the world and brought economic sanctions to an end. Similarly, a new democratic political climate in Chile precipitated the leaping advances in the country's wine industry in the 80s. For a while it seemed that these two countries had missed the boat. In the mid 90s both were associated with basic supermarket wines of inferior quality to those produced in Australia and New Zealand. Today, though Chile and South Africa do produce some simple, inexpensive wines, this is not the end of the story.

Reds
Mid-price Chilean Carmenere + mid-price South African Cabernet or Cabernet-based blend + mid-

Here's an idea for you

Both Carmenere and Pinotage make excellent partners for food, particularly grilled red meat. Try experimenting in matching their pronounced flavours with dishes that you might otherwise serve with Cabernet or Pinot Noir.

price Pinotage + similarly priced Cabernet-based Bordeaux + similarly priced Californian Cabernet

Whites
Mid-price Chilean Chardonnay + mid-price South African Chardonnay + mid-price Chilean Sauvignon Blanc+ expensive New Zealand Sauvignon Blanc + mid-price Australian Chardonnay

Some of the wines that you've tasted may have seemed very similar in style. Perhaps you felt that they simply tasted like very typical New World Chardonnay, Sauvignon or Cabernet. There is an argument that with the growing globalisation of the wine industry the origin of a wine is becoming less important. At a fundamental level this seems a valid argument; basic Chilean Chardonnay won't taste much different from Chardonnay made in South Africa, Australia or northern Italy. At a more elevated level, the discovery of new regions that are well suited to certain grape varieties has created wines with unique qualities, such as Chardonnays from the South African region of Robertson and wonderfully glossy Cabernets from Rapel in Chile.

It is with offbeat grapes that regions such as South Africa and Chile are creating their own identity. Both Chile and South Africa have wines that they've succeeded in making their own. In Chile there's Carmenere – which probably originated from Bordeaux – and Pinotage, a hybrid grape created by crossing Pinot Noir with Cinsault.

40. The lure of the Loire

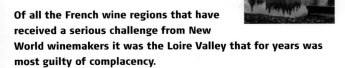

Of all the French wine regions that have received a serious challenge from New World winemakers it was the Loire Valley that for years was most guilty of complacency.

When winemakers in the Loire woke up to the fact that their wines were being eclipsed by New World upstarts, from New Zealand in particular, they quickly began to clean up their act. In the finest cases the new generation of Loire Sauvignons – notably Pouilly Fume and Sancerre – offer the best of both worlds: they combine the freshness of New Zealand Sauvignon with the minerally grace and charm associated with many of the best French wines.

Taste Test
Inexpensive Touraine Sauvignon + inexpensive Chilean Sauvignon + inexpensive New Zealand Sauvignon + good-quality Sancerre or Pouilly Fume + good-quality New Zealand Sauvignon Blanc

Here's an idea for you

The Loire is a complex wine region that requires a detailed map to help you find the places behind the names. Whenever tasting a wine from the Loire ensure that you have located its precise location on a map.

Defining idea

In this test you should see Sauvignon
in its multitude of different guises,
which can range from thin and
watery to rich, opulent and three-
dimensional. Which do you like most
and which do you think offer the best
value for money?

For many accustomed to the assertive flavours of New World whites,
Muscadet (Melon de Bourgogne) might seem a little restrained, but serve
it with seafood or subtle fish dishes and you may think differently. The
other major white grape variety, Chenin Blanc (Vouvray), might have a
poor reputation outside the Loire but it is really the grape with which
producers excel. The most successful red grape variety, Cabernet Franc
(Chinon and Bourgueil), is becoming increasingly popular in the New
World, but don't overlook those from the Loire; they are exceptionally
good value for money and a superb accompaniment to food.

To put the wines into context try the following line-ups:

- Good-quality Muscadet + basic Chilean Sauvignon Blanc + basic
  northern Italian white
- Good-quality medium sweet Vouvray + Alsace Gewurztraminer +
  inexpensive Australian Chardonnay
- Chinon or Bourgueil Cabernet Franc + Australian Shiraz

41. Take me to the river

The vineyards that stretch down to the Rhône produce some of the world's most robust but delicious reds – and also one of the most legendary whites.

The Rhône's greatest success has been to remain true to its winemaking tradition in the face of competition from New World wines. While winemakers in other French wine regions have tried to mimic the hugely successful style of Australian Shiraz (a wine made from the Rhône's classic red grape, Syrah), the Rhône's have made a huge effort to improve what they were already doing – with stunning results.

The northern Rhône is where the Syrah grape holds sway, producing fabulous individual wines such as Cote Rotie, Hermitage, St Joseph, Crozes Hermitage and Cornas. It's also here that the white Viognier grape has its spiritual home in the tiny appellation of Condrieu, where it makes magnificent sensual wines with an almost mythical reputation.

Here's an idea for you

Hearty Rhône reds aren't made to be drunk on their own – compare your reactions to a Rhône red, first by tasting it alone and then in the company of food. You'll be amazed at the difference.

Defining idea

'What the superior man seeks is in himself: what the small man seeks is in others.'
CONFUCIUS, Analects

As the river heads to the warmer south, the wines get beefier, ranging from simple Cotes du Rhône to complex Chateauneuf du Pape. These derive much of their charm from the fact that they are made from a range of grapes, including Mourvedre, Cinsault and Carignan.

The following tasting will demonstrate the variety of styles offered by the region:
Good-quality Hermitage + good-quality Chateauneuf du Pape + good-quality Cotes du Rhône + basic Cotes du Rhône + good-quality Australian Shiraz + inexpensive Australian Cabernet Sauvignon

Although the Syrah grape dominates the Rhône, the region's wines are not about grapes – they are about rich flavours, sun and soil. Nevertheless, comparing them closely with single-variety wines such as Australian Cabernet Sauvignon and Shiraz should make you see them in a very different light.

The style of Rhône wines has been widely copied by a number of New World producers. In California, Rhône-style blends offer an alternative to the monotony of single-variety reds such as Cabernet and Merlot, and in South Africa one producer has been so keen to pay homage to the region that he has produced a wine called Goats du Roam.

42. Burgundy

When you first stumble upon a good one you will come to realise that tasting and smelling great red Burgundy is a life-changing experience.

But taste a bad red Burgundy and you might be left wondering what all the fuss is about. There is no doubt that much of the grape's appeal lies in its inconsistency. For many wine lovers, finding good red Burgundy is like finding truffles – it combines gastronomy with thrill of the chase. For winemakers it offers a similar challenge. This notoriously fickle grape variety is the petulant prima donna of the grape world and can create good and bad wines in equal measure.

To hardened old-school wine buffs the vineyards of the Cote d'Or are the only places where it's possible to make truly great Pinot Noir. Yet despite the grape's reputation a number of winemakers in other wine regions with a similarly cool, temperate climate, such as in New Zealand, Australia, Oregon, California and Germany, have had a great success in creating fabulous perfumed wines with this grape.

Here's an idea for you

However disappointing basic red Burgundy might appear on first taste, it is a good example of a French wine that tastes far better with food than on its own. Try drinking it with a typical dish of the region such as boeuf bourguignon.

103

Taste Test – reds

Good-quality red Burgundy + basic red Burgundy + good-quality New Zealand Pinot Noir + good-quality Pinot Noir from either California or Oregon

There is a high chance that the wines in this tasting will lead you to conclude that in the right hands and the right conditions the Pinot Noir grape can be used to make great wines anywhere in the world.

The Cote de Beaune is to Chardonnay what the Cote d'Or is to Pinot Noir. But to buy the wines at their best you need to dig deep into your pocket. However, Chardonnay is a more versatile grape than Pinot Noir and creates a much wider range of styles, from simple and refreshing to impressively complex.

Taste Test – whites

Good-quality white Burgundy + good-quality Californian Chardonnay + mid-range South African Chardonnay

How does breathtakingly expensive white Burgundy stand up to the competition? Even if it is better, is it worth the extra investment? Though inexpensive white Burgundy can be very disappointing, many would opt for the good-value whites to be found further south in the Maconnais. These offer the combination of the prestige of white Burgundy with crisp, racy flavours.

43. The reign of terroir

Is the idea of terroir nothing more than a figment of French winemakers' imagination? An excuse for badly made, earthy wines?

The idea of terroir is tied up with the French belief that wine is primarily the gift of nature rather than of people. As such, this notion is the polar opposite of the New World philosophy that wine is primarily the product of gleaming, temperature-controlled fermentation tanks.

To understand terroir it helps to look at it in the context of French gastronomy, where the emphasis is on local ingredients. To the average French citizen, food is a reflection of the environment in which it was grown – and usually, thanks to a sense of local pride, the meat, fruit and vegetables grown in your own neighbourhood are perceived as the best. The same goes for wine: it is defined not by grape but by where it comes from – Bordeaux, Loire, Rhône, Burgundy.

Here's an idea for you

If you need convincing about the influence that the weather and soil has on plant life, examine the difference in the flavours of the same variety of apples grown in different areas of the world.

Defining idea

'*Man masters nature not by force but by understanding.*'
ROBERT BRIDGES

To the detractors of traditional French winemaking, this attitude explains the poor quality of much of its output. French winemakers, they believe, simply plant the vines and let nature do the rest. The result is poor grapes and limp, dirty-tasting wines. Although this might have been the approach of some winemakers in the dim past, it is certainly not true today, and it is quite possible to believe in both the concept of terroir and good winemaking.

The belief in terroir has spread beyond France. As winemaking in Australia, California and South Africa becomes ever more sophisticated, winemakers are discovering that, far from being a far-fetched concept, terroir helps to explain the shades of difference between the wines made in different vineyards. So they are now identifying the areas that produce the best grapes – a practice that's having a huge impact on the quality of the wines.

In general, the more expensive the wine the more likely it is to offer a sense of place. However, there are plenty of expensive wines that could be made anywhere in the world and plenty of cheap wines that eloquently express a sense of place.

44. The great white hope

The Semillon grape makes some of the world's most alluring wines. Allow its enticing flavours and aromas to enhance your gastronomic life.

Few grapes reward perseverance like Semillon. With experience what once might have seemed flabby begins to seem rich and opulent and in some cases utterly beguiling, especially with age.

There is no doubt that Semillon is the unsung hero of white grapes. In combination with Sauvignon Blanc it is used to make Sauternes, arguably the greatest sweet white wine in the world; one whose flavours respond beautifully to botrytis, the mould that forms when the grapes rot. Semillon plays a similar role in white Bordeaux and also as a partner to Chardonnay in many New World blends.

Here's an idea for you

Try experimenting with the different styles of Semillon in conjunction with a variety of different foods. Try drinking a dry white Semillon-based Bordeaux with fish and seafood, or sweet Semillon with rich, creamy puddings and blue cheese. Semillon can also make a great partner to spicy food.

While Semillon is often used to make lacklustre wines in France, in its new spiritual home in Australia's Hunter Valley the grape puts on a virtuoso performance in extraordinarily rich, nutty dry whites, the first taste of which can completely transform one's whole attitude to white wine. In the cooler areas of Australia, Semillon is used to produce wines with a fresher, grassier character reminiscent of Sauvignon Blanc. With four to five years' ageing it becomes even more intriguing and complex.

However, it seems unlikely that Semillon will ever have mass appeal. Like Pinot Noir and Riesling its style can be so inconsistent that for many people the first taste is also the last. But perseverance will pay huge dividends.

Try the following Taste Test and you could find yourself at the start of a lifelong relationship:
Hunter Valley Semillon + Semillon-based white Bordeaux + Semillon from a cool Australian region such as Tasmania + Australian blend of Chardonnay and Semillon + Sauternes + good-quality Australian Chardonnay + good-quality New Zealand Sauvignon Blanc

You should now have tasted the Semillon grape in a variety of different incarnations – on its own, blended with Sauvignon Blanc and as a sweet white wine. Even if you didn't find a style that you liked, try persevering, particularly with examples from Australia.

45. The heat is on

Temperature plays a key role in the way that a wine expresses itself. Instead of adhering to prescriptive guidelines, chuck away the rulebook and discover what works best for you.

Try one glass of your favourite Champagne chilled until it is almost freezing and one glass of the same Champagne which is neither warm nor cold. Focus on the aroma and then the flavour of the wine in each of the glasses. Which has the greatest smell and which has the greatest flavour? Which is the most refreshing? It's worth trying the experiment with a variety of other wines, both red and white.

The ability to judge the optimum temperature for a wine is the result of a combination of common sense and experience in equal measure:

■ The temperature of a bottle after it has been in the fridge for a few hours tends to be ideal.

Here's an idea for you

For a few days try to taste wines at different temperatures. Keep the remnants of a bottle of red Bordeaux in the fridge and try it the next day. How does chilling affect Sauternes or Port? The more you experiment the more you'll be able to hone your judgement.

- Putting a white wine in the freezer for a few minutes is a hopelessly inexact means of chilling it.
- If you want to chill a bottle of Champagne, do so in a bucket filled with ice and water rather than in the freezer. The latter will inevitably chill it until it is too cold, or worse still, waste the contents by freezing it.
- Similarly, the practice of placing a bottle of wine near a range cooker, stove or radiator is a hopelessly imprecise way to get the wine to the correct temperature.
- The most ludicrous piece of advice on temperature is that some wines should be served at 'room temperature'. What sort of room? A centrally heated, hermetically sealed apartment? Or a chilly country house?

The idea that red wines should always be served a few degrees below tepid suggests that there are no red wines suitable for summer drinking. Nothing could be further from the truth. There are plenty of reds – such as Gamay and those from the Loire – that lend themselves to being served at the same temperature at which you would serve a dry white wine.

46. Break for the Bordeaux

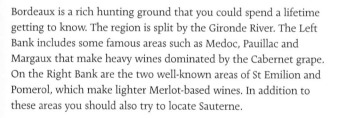

Bordeaux might be the most complex, confusing wine region in the world, but persevere and you will be rewarded with the most magnificent, subtle wines known to humankind.

Bordeaux is a rich hunting ground that you could spend a lifetime getting to know. The region is split by the Gironde River. The Left Bank includes some famous areas such as Medoc, Pauillac and Margaux that make heavy wines dominated by the Cabernet grape. On the Right Bank are the two well-known areas of St Emilion and Pomerol, which make lighter Merlot-based wines. In addition to these areas you should also try to locate Sauterne.

The reason that Bordeaux has had such a long tradition of creating fabulous wines is that it has the happy combination of well-drained soil that is heated by the Mediterranean and cooled by the Atlantic. Between the 1850s and the 1950s many of Bordeaux's vineyards were classified in a number of different strata. The

Here's an idea for you

You'll learn more about the distinctive character of Bordeaux by regular, simple blind tasting that compares just two wines – a red Bordeaux and, say, a Shiraz, Chianti or Rhône.

first classification in 1855 – of most of the Left Bank – still influences wine prices 150 years later. Free-thinking drinkers, however, tend to trust their taste buds rather than ludicrously outdated wine parades.

The red wines are made primarily from Cabernet Sauvignon and Merlot as well as a smaller proportion of other grapes such as Cabernet Franc, Petit Verdot and Malbec. The best-known sweet wines are made in Sauternes, and the best-known white wines are made in Graves and Entre-deux-mers. Bordeaux is such a vast area with so many producers that it offers a huge variety of styles in any given year. The only dependable gauges of quality are your taste buds and your nose.

Taste Test – reds
Good-quality Cabernet-based red from Medoc + good-quality Merlot-based red from St Emilion or Pomerol + cheap basic red Bordeaux + good-quality aged Rioja + good-quality Australian Cabernet + good-quality Chilean Merlot

How did the Bordeaux wines compare with those from other parts of the world? Did you detect a similarity among the Bordeaux wines?

Taste Test – whites
Cheap white Bordeaux + expensive white Bordeaux + New Zealand Sauvignon Blanc + Australian Semillon

What differences in style did you notice among these wines?

47. Many happy returns?

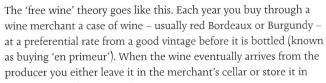

For some wine buffs, buying wine and selling it a few years later at a profit is a crafty way of helping to fund their drinking habits. Well, that's the theory anyway...

The 'free wine' theory goes like this. Each year you buy through a wine merchant a case of wine – usually red Bordeaux or Burgundy – at a preferential rate from a good vintage before it is bottled (known as buying 'en primeur'). When the wine eventually arrives from the producer you either leave it in the merchant's cellar or store it in your own. In a few years' time, when the wine has reached maturity you sell half the wine at a profit, which you use to buy some more wine before it is bottled, and drink the rest.

It sounds simple, doesn't it? But just bear in mind the following pitfalls and hidden costs:

Here's an idea for you

Before embarking on the arduous business of buying and selling wines, make sure that you are certain that you are wedded to aged wines. Even if you are, are there qualities in old wines that you might possibly find in less expensive vintages than those from Bordeaux and Burgundy?

Defining idea

'You don't get owt for nowt.'
Old northern English saying

■ The price at which the wine is advertised by the producer looks attractive, but by the time it reaches you or the wine merchant it will have attracted taxes additional to that price.

■ If you decide to keep the wine on the merchant's premises you will have to pay a storage charge. There's also a possibility that if the merchant goes bust you could lose all your wine.

■ Even if you have enough space with the right conditions for storing wine, there's the chance that they could be stolen or that your cellar could be damaged by a fire or a flood.

■ The wine might fail to fulfil its potential and therefore offer little if any return on your investment.

With so many potential pitfalls and overheads, the risks seem high and the potential returns slim. Remember too that in what are thought to be very good vintages competition for wines is intense and so prices rise dramatically and offer very little potential for significant returns for many years to come.

48. Beyond Liebfraumilch

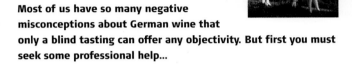

Most of us have so many negative misconceptions about German wine that only a blind tasting can offer any objectivity. But first you must seek some professional help...

Thin, mean and tasteless, in the 70s German wines fuelled institutional functions, where their only attraction appeared to be that they were cold and wet – and very, very cheap. But poor quality is just one of Germany's catalogue of woes. In the brave new wine world where the fashion is for dry styles of wines with a hint of fruitiness and with labels that are easy to understand, the idiosyncratic style of many German wines and their ludicrous gradations of style and quality and austere-looking labels make them a marketing executive's nightmare. However energetically one might trumpet the revival of interest in Riesling, most consumers still remember their first taste of German wine and opt instead for the sunny flavours of Chardonnay.

Here's an idea for you

Rather than serving Champagne before a meal, try offering a good dry Riesling as an alternative. Its assertive style is perfect for stimulating the appetite – and it's much better value for money.

115

Defining idea

'A German wine label is one thing that life's too short for, a daunting testimony to that peculiar nation's love of details and organisation.'
KINGSLEY AMIS

It gets worse. In the same way that they have exploited classic French grapes such as Sauvignon Blanc, Shiraz, Semillon, Cabernet and, of course, Chardonnay, New World winemakers have also succeeded in making Riesling with greater appeal and approachability than have winemakers in its spiritual home.

Don't even try to master the litany of Tafelwein, Landwein, QbA and QmPs. Simply enlist the help of a wine merchant. If there's one thing that wine merchants love, it's an underdog – and top of their list of underdogs is Germany. For very nerdy wine merchants, one of the great attractions of German winemaking is its impenetrability. They will love showing off their intimate knowledge of the subject. So use it. Limit yourself to just one grape: Riesling. Ask your friendly merchant to suggest wines that fit the following descriptions and then compare them against each other.

Cheap German Riesling + good-quality dry German Riesling + good-quality medium sweet German Riesling + good-quality dry Australian Riesling + good-quality expensive New Zealand Riesling + Sauternes + inexpensive Australian Chardonnay

49. Local heroes

Some of the best wines have an extra dimension: as well as being delicious they also express the winemaking tradition of the area where they were made. And they needn't cost the earth.

Wine falls into two categories: the stuff that reflects the winemaking tradition of the region where it was produced and the sort that tastes as though it could have been made anywhere in the world where the sun shines enough to ripen grapes. What sets these two kinds of wine apart is something that wine buffs called 'typicity' – the quality of conforming to a certain style that is typical of the wine's birthplace.

While the consistency of 'global' wines might offer a convenient option for everyday drinking, the highs and lows are provided by wines that taste of the place they come from. The people of every region of the world have their own tastes in food and these are

Here's an idea for you

Typical wines tend to be part of a gastronomic tradition. Try drinking wines that are typical of an area with corresponding regional specialities, e.g. bold southern French red with cassoulet, and Muscadet with seafood.

influenced by the available ingredients, the climate and the gastronomic tradition that has evolved over the years. Precisely the same is true of wine. Though terroir does contribute to the sense of place, the typicity suggested by the wine has much to do with winemaking tradition – the style of wine created by techniques such as oak ageing and blending.

To distinguish between these two kinds of wine try comparing inexpensive Chilean Merlot and good-quality Rioja, for the reds, and inexpensive Chilean Sauvignon Blanc and good-quality Sancerre, for the whites. In each case, ask yourself which of the two wines in the glasses before you could have been made anywhere in the world and which has an idiosyncratic feel that is all its own.

Although it is easy to see typicity as a quality that is peculiar to European wine regions such as France, Italy and Spain, some New World areas are developing their own styles and winemaking traditions. For instance Sauvignon Blanc from Marlborough in New Zealand tastes very different from Sauvignon from Western Australia, and Barossa Shiraz has a style different from Shiraz made in South Africa.

50. Keeping your palate on its toes

Even when you're focusing on a limited number of grape varieties and styles, it's useful to venture occasionally into uncharted territory.

There are a huge number of wines that no one except a few hardened wine buffs is aware of. Plenty of wines are made purely for local consumption. Though initially you should keep these kinds of wines at arm's length, they will be essential for pushing your taste buds to the extremes – just as the best fitness training programme will exercise muscles that you don't normally use. The chances are that you won't like them. But they will offer flavours and aromas that your palate and nose wouldn't otherwise be subjected to. They will stretch your senses to the extremes of their experience.

The secret to tasting such wines is never to get too involved. You don't need to know a great deal about wine in order to enjoy it. What is far more important is that you, your palate and your nose are

Here's an idea for you

Next time you visit a Greek, Lebanese or Turkish restaurant try to sample the local wines on offer. These restaurants will also give you the opportunity to taste the wines in a gastronomic context where they might not taste quite so weird.

Defining idea

'One should try everything once, except incest and folk-dancing.'
SIR ARNOLD BAX

receptive to them. If you find an offbeat wine that you like, that might be the time to investigate the winemaking tradition from which it springs.

For some really extreme experiences, try wines made from local grape varieties.

- **Austria**: Gruner Veltliner might twist the tongue – but its taste should keep it on its toes too.
- **England**: varieties such as Seyval Banc, Schonburger, Huxelrebe, Bacchus, Kerner and Ortega can't fail to stimulate the palate.
- **Germany**: try Scheurebe Silvaner, Lemberger and Dornfelder.
- **Greece**: try the native Greek varieties such as Agiorgitiko.
- **Mexico**: try the fabulous, obscure Petite Sirah grape, which will put predictable Cabernet in the shade.
- **Switzerland**: go off piste with local specialities such as Chasselas, Arvine and Amigne.

51. Avoiding hangovers

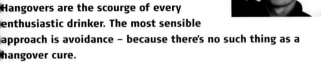

Hangovers are the scourge of every enthusiastic drinker. The most sensible approach is avoidance – because there's no such thing as a hangover cure.

For the free-thinking drinker, wine is not about intoxication – it's about appreciating subtle flavours and aromas. If you're taking part in a gastronomic session that involves matching different wines with different courses, make sure that you don't drink more than half a glass of each – to enjoy a wine you don't need to drink a huge quantity of it – just enough to savour.

Plenty of water is essential before and during a tasting session – partly because it acts as a brake on the amount of wine that you can drink and partly because it counters the diuretic effect of alcohol. Drink at least a large glass of water for every small glass of

Here's an idea for you

Many wine buffs keep a few bottles of wine open at the same time – partly so that they can compare them and also so that they can try them out with different foods. On a day-to-day basis this practice can encourage you to simply *taste* a couple of wines rather than open a bottle and finish it within a day or two.

Defining idea

'My view is that the golden rule in life is never to have too much of anything.'
TERENCE

wine you drink. Water is also a good way of cleansing you palate in preparation for the next wine.

The better the wines you drink, the less likely you are to feel the consequences the morning after. The other advantage of good-quality wine is that it tends to be more satisfying, so you aren't tempted to drink more than you need.

Much of the damage is done in the last throes of a meal. Try to avoid the following:

- Coffee. Alcohol does enough damage to your sleep patterns. Why make them even worse?
- More than one glass of Port. Either drink port when you are sober or drink it sparingly if you are mildly drunk. It might slip down easily but it has an alcohol content of 19%.
- Spirits. Is the end of a meal really the time to enjoy your prized single malt? If anything, it should be deployed as an early-evening aperitif when you aren't planning to do much drinking.

52. Vinous nirvana

Simply following the advice here won't guarantee that you'll become a free-thinking drinker in a flash. But if you persist you'll be handsomely rewarded with a lifetime of pleasure.

However, the more that you taste, the more that you'll begin to trust your own instincts. Then one day you'll pull the cork on a bottle of obscure or little-loved wine, taste it, love it and – most importantly – shout your enthusiasm from the rooftops without fear of embarrassment. That is the hallmark of vinous nirvana. This new dimension of your appreciation of wine will enable you to drink wine without fear of embarrassment and to say when it's good, bad or corked.

Five signs that you're a free-thinking drinker

. You don't judge a wine by its fancy bottle.

. You serve unusual, offbeat wines with confidence.

. You question the opinions of

Here's an idea for you

Start testing your opinions on someone who was at the same stage you were at before you embarked on your present exploration of wine. Pour a glass of a well-known wine (be sure to make its identity clear) and ask her to talk about it. Compare what she has to say with you own thoughts. Haven't you come a long way?

wine buffs, wine merchants and sommeliers.
4. You express your vinous opinions with confidence.
5. Your decisions to serve certain wines with different sorts of food are based on your own experience.

However, the more you know about wine, the greater the danger that you might become more interested in the detail than in the bigger picture.

Five signs that you're becoming a bore
1. You develop an unhealthy interest in the way that wine is made.
2. You start buying tickets to vertical tastings that allow you to compare the differences between a range of vintages of the same wine.
3. You become obsessed with a wine's failings rather than its attractions.
4. You come up with phrases such as 'Wow, get a load of that yeasty autolysis'.
5. You become more interested in experts' opinions rather than your own.

Free-thinking drinking is not about taking wine lightly; but about not letting your instincts be clouded by issues that don't matter. Try to remember the joy you felt when you first tasted a wine and found it truly delicious. How much did that pleasure have to do with your knowledge of how or where it was made? The secret to vinous nirvana is more about what you *feel* than what you *know*.

brilliant ideas

This book is published by Infinite Ideas, creators of the acclaimed **52 Brilliant Ideas** series. If you found this book helpful, here are some other titles in the **Brilliant Little Ideas** series which you may also find interesting.

- **Be incredibly healthy:** 52 brilliant little ideas to look and feel fantastic
- **Create your dream house and garden:** 52 brilliant little ideas for big home improvements
- **Enjoy great sleep:** 52 brilliant little ideas for bedtime bliss
- **Find your dream job:** 52 brilliant little ideas for total career success
- **Get fit:** 52 brilliant little ideas to win at the gym
- **Get rid of your gut:** 52 brilliant little ideas for a sensational six pack
- **Quit smoking for good:** 52 brilliant little ideas to kick the habit
- **Relax:** 52 brilliant little ideas to chill out
- **Rescue our world:** 52 brilliant little ideas to save the planet
- **Seduce anyone:** 52 brilliant little ideas for being incredibly sexy
- **Shape up your life:** 52 brilliant little ideas for becoming the person you want to be
- **Win at winter sports:** 52 brilliant little ideas for skiing and snowboarding

For more detailed information on these books and others published by Infinite Ideas please visit www.infideas.com.

See reverse for order form.

Qty	Title	RRP
	Be incredibly creative	£4.99
	Create your dream house & garden	£4.99
	Enjoy great sleep	£5.99
	Find your dream job	£5.99
	Get fit	£5.99
	Get rid of your gut	£4.99
	Quit smoking for good	£4.99
	Relax	£5.99
	Rescue our world	£4.99
	Seduce anyone	£5.99
	Shape up your life	£5.99
	Win at winter sports	£4.99

Add £2.49 postage per delivery address

TOTAL

Name: ....

Delivery address: ....

....

....

E-mail:.............................Tel (in case of problems): ....

By post Fill in all relevant details, cut out or copy this page and send along with a cheque made payable to Infinite Ideas. Send to: *Brilliant Little Ideas*, Infinite Ideas, 36 St Giles, Oxford OX1 3LD. **Credit card orders over the telephone** Call +44 (0) 1865 514 888. Lines are open 9am to 5pm Monday to Friday.

Please note that no payment will be processed until your order has been dispatched. Goods are dispatched through Royal Mail within 14 working days, when in stock. We never forward personal details on to third parties or bombard you with junk mail. The prices quoted are for UK and RoI residents only. If you are outside these areas please contact us for postage and packing rates. Any questions or comments please contact us on 01865 514 888 or email info@infideas.com.